A Guide to
AMERICAN STATES

Wyoming

THE EQUALITY STATE

MEDIA ENHANCED BOOKS
AV²
BY WEIGL
ADDED VALUE • AUDIO VISUAL

www.av2books.com

AV² provides enriched content that supplements and complements this book. Weigl's AV² books strive to create inspired learning and engage young minds in a total learning experience.

Your AV² Media Enhanced books come alive with...

Audio
Listen to sections of the book read aloud.

Key Words
Study vocabulary, and complete a matching word activity.

Video
Watch informative video clips.

Quizzes
Test your knowledge.

Embedded Weblinks
Gain additional information for research.

Slide Show
View images and captions, and prepare a presentation.

Try This!
Complete activities and hands-on experiments.

... and much, much more!

Go to **www.av2books.com**, and enter this book's unique code.

BOOK CODE

N 4 1 5 3 3 2

AV² by Weigl brings you media enhanced books that support active learning.

Published by AV² by Weigl
350 5th Avenue, 59th Floor
New York, NY 10118
Website: www.av2books.com   www.weigl.com

Library of Congress Cataloging-in-Publication Data

Parker, Janice.
  Wyoming / Janice Parker.
     p. cm. -- (A guide to American states)
Includes index.
ISBN 978-1-61690-824-9 (hardcover : alk. paper) -- ISBN 978-1-61690-499-9 (online)
1. Wyoming--Juvenile literature. I. Title.
  F761.3.P373 2011
  978.7--dc23
                          2011019240

Printed in the United States of America in North Mankato, Minnesota

052011
WEP180511

Project Coordinator Jordan McGill
Art Director Terry Paulhus

Photo Credits
Every reasonable effort has been made to trace ownership and to obtain permission to reprint copyright material. The publishers would be pleased to have any errors or omissions brought to their attention so that they may be corrected in subsequent printings.

Weigl acknowledges Getty Images as its primary image supplier for this title.
Photo of Abraham Lincoln Presidential Library and Museum on page 20 courtesy of Edward A. Thomas.

Contents

How Devils Tower formed is a mystery. It looks like the top of an ancient volcano. However, there is no good evidence of volcanic activity surrounding it.

Introduction

"Nature had collected all of her beauties together in one chosen place." Explorer John C. Frémont's description of Wyoming's landscape when he first set eyes on it in 1842 still rings true today. Since Frémont's time, many other visitors have admired the region's remarkable natural beauty, and many people have made the state their home.

Wyoming's natural attractions include Grand Teton National Park and Devils Tower. The 1,267-foot Devils Tower is a sacred site of worship for many American Indians. According to legend, the marks on the side of the huge rock were made by the claws of a giant bear. Wyoming's inspirational landscape also has a special place in U.S.

Wyoming is also known as the Cowboy State. This nickname pays tribute to the early ranchers and pioneers.

Fossil Butte National Monument is located in Wyoming. Covering nearly 8,200 acres, the site features fossils of plants and animals that lived in the region more than 50 million years ago.

history. Most of Yellowstone National Park is located in the state, and Yellowstone was the first national park created by the U.S. government.

Much of Wyoming's terrain is rugged, which posed a challenge for the thousands of early pioneers who traveled through the region. For those pioneers who first settled in the area, a lack of good cropland made it difficult to earn a living. Today, however, Wyoming has a highly developed ranching tradition and is one of the country's most attractive recreational states. Its many lakes and rivers are used for boating and fishing. Forests full of plant and animal life attract hunters and wildlife observers. The mountains and parks are popular destinations for campers, hikers, and backpackers.

Where Is Wyoming?

Wyoming is located in the western United States. During Wyoming's pioneer days, it was an essential corridor to the West. Most of the historic trails to the West cut through Wyoming. The Oregon, California, and **Mormon** trails brought settlers through the South Pass of the Continental Divide in west-central Wyoming.

Each year, approximately 2.5 million people visit Grand Teton National Park. The park is named for the Grand Teton, which is the tallest peak in the Teton Mountains. The Grand Teton is 13,770 feet above sea level.

The Continental Divide is an imaginary line that runs from Alaska and Canada through the western states and the western side of South America. It is also known as the Great Divide. Rivers on the east of the divide flow toward the Gulf of Mexico and the Atlantic Ocean. Rivers on the western side flows to the Pacific Ocean and Gulf of California. In Wyoming, the Continental Divide stretches from the south-central part of the state up through the northwest, leaving the state through Yellowstone National Park.

Wyoming is accessible to travelers by highways and by air. Casper has an international airport. County and regional airports service various locations, such as Jackson Hole and Laramie. There is even an airport inside Yellowstone National Park.

I DIDN'T KNOW THAT!

Wyoming has a land area of approximately 97,100 square miles. It is the ninth-largest state in land area.

The highest peak in the state is Gannett Peak. It is 13,804 feet above sea level. Gannett Peak has glaciers on both its northern and eastern faces.

The lowest point in Wyoming is on the Belle Fourche River. It is 3,010 feet above sea level.

Wagon ruts from the historic Oregon Trail can still be seen in Wyoming. The trail, which was about 2,000 miles long, extended from Missouri to Oregon.

Mapping Wyoming

Wyoming is bordered by Montana to the north and northwest, South Dakota and Nebraska to the east, Colorado to the south, Utah to the southwest, and Idaho to the west. Getting around by land vehicle is relatively easy. Wyoming has an extensive network of state and federal roads. Interstate 25 runs north–south through the middle of the state. Interstate 80 runs east–west. Interstate 90 runs east–west in the northeast corner.

Sites and Symbols

STATE SEAL
Wyoming

STATE BIRD
Meadowlark

STATE FLOWER
Indian Paintbrush

STATE FLAG
Wyoming

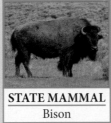

STATE MAMMAL
Bison

STATE TREE
Plains Cottonwood

Nickname Equality State, Cowboy State, Big Wyoming

Motto Equal Rights

Song "Wyoming," words by C. E. Winter and music by G.E. Knapp.

Entered the Union July 10, 1890, as the 44th state

Capital Cheyenne

Population (2010 Census) 563,626 Ranked 50th state

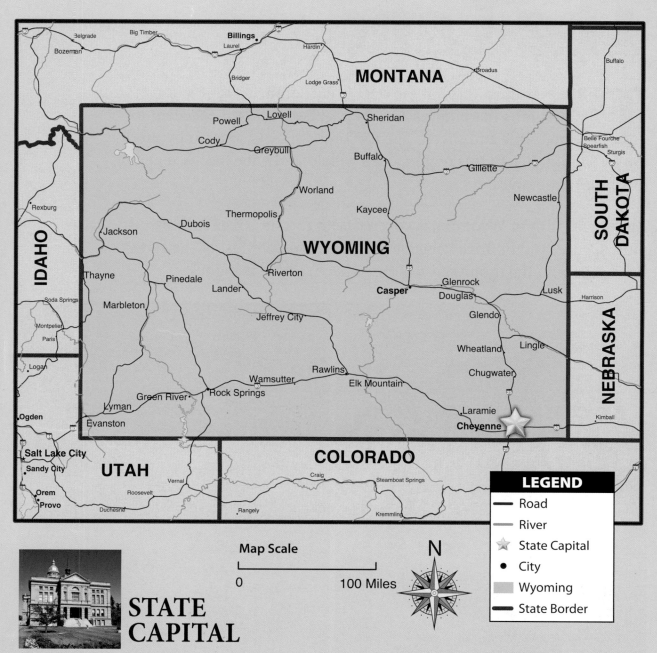

MONTANA

WYOMING

IDAHO

SOUTH DAKOTA

NEBRASKA

UTAH

COLORADO

Belgrade
Big Timber
Billings
Laurel
Hardin
Bozeman
Bridger
Lodge Grass
Buffalo
Powell
Lovell
Sheridan
Cody
Greybull
Buffalo
Gillette
Belle Fourche
Spearfish
Sturgis
Rexburg
Worland
Newcastle
Thermopolis
Kaycee
Jackson
Dubois
Thayne
Pinedale
Riverton
Glenrock
Lusk
Harrison
Soda Springs
Lander
Casper
Douglas
Marbleton
Jeffrey City
Glendo
Montpelier
Paris
Wheatland
Lingle
Logan
Rawlins
Chugwater
Wamsutter
Elk Mountain
Ogden
Green River
Rock Springs
Laramie
Kimball
Lyman
Evanston
Cheyenne
Salt Lake City
Sandy City
Craig
Steamboat Springs
Vernal
Orem
Roosevelt
Provo
Duchesne
Rangely
Kremmling

LEGEND

───	Road
───	River
★	State Capital
●	City
�Wyoming▮	Wyoming
━━━	State Border

Map Scale

0   100 Miles

N

STATE CAPITAL

Wyoming's **capitol** in Cheyenne was built to resemble the U.S. Capitol in Washington, D.C. Its construction was authorized in 1886, and the cornerstone was laid the following year. Additional wings were completed in 1890 and 1917. Local flagstone was used for the foundation, and local sandstone was used for the upper floors. Inside each chamber, there is a stained glass ceiling with the state seal in the center.

United States

Hawai'i   Alaska

Wyoming

The Land

The easternmost third of the state is part of the Great Plains. This region's flat prairies and short grasses make it excellent for raising cattle and sheep. The rest of the state is covered by the Rocky Mountains. In this region, deep valleys and wide basins separate the mountain ranges.

About one-fifth of Wyoming is covered with forests. Trees such as pine, spruce, and fir are a valuable natural resource. Most of the state's forests grow in the mountain regions, where rainfall is highest.

DEVILS TOWER

In 1906, President Theodore Roosevelt declared Devils Tower the first U.S. national monument. He wanted to protect the landform and thought that Congress might take too long to make it a national park.

TETON MOUNTAINS

When land shifts around large cracks in Earth's crust, it is called faulting. The Teton Mountains are one of the best examples of block faulting. Stress inside Earth caused huge blocks of rock to tilt up. These landforms are called block mountains, or horsts.

AYRES NATURAL BRIDGE

Ayres Natural Bridge in Wyoming is one of the few natural bridges in the world to have water flowing under it.

SHOSHONE NATIONAL FOREST

Shoshone National Forest was the first national forest. It was designated a national forest in 1891 by President Benjamin Harris.

Connecticut, Delaware, Hawaii, Maryland, Massachusetts, New Hampshire, New Jersey, Rhode Island, Vermont, and West Virginia could all fit within Wyoming's borders at the same time.

Modern ranger stations in the state and national parks and forests are part house and part office. Wyoming was, in fact, the first state to construct a ranger station. It was built in 1891, the same year Shoshone National Forest was established as a protected area.

Grand Teton National Park was formed north of Jackson Hole, a northwestern valley, to help protect the area from commercial development. Oil **magnate** John D. Rockefeller bought up much of the land and then donated it. Today, only 3 percent of land in the Jackson Hole area is privately owned.

The people who live in the Jackson Hole area and elsewhere in Wyoming are used to weather reports with wide-ranging highs and lows. The mountain ranges stop wind from stirring the air in the valleys. This effect allows colder air to drop into the valleys.

Climate

Temperatures can vary in different areas of Wyoming because of differences in elevation. In many areas, average high July temperatures range from 85° Fahrenheit to 95° F. But in the mountains, the average July maximum temperature is closer to 70° F. The greatest amount of rain and snow falls in the mountains, while the plains receive little precipitation. Wyoming's highest recorded temperature occurred in Basin on August 8, 1983, when the thermometer hit 115° F. The lowest known temperature was recorded at Riverside on February 9, 1933. It was –66° F. Wyoming is one of the windiest states in the United States. Winds often reach 30 to 40 miles per hour, or mph. Gusts of wind often register at 50 to 60 mph.

Average Annual Temperatures Across Wyoming

Lake Yellowstone is in the northwest corner of the state. It is the largest freshwater lake above 7,000 feet in North America. Ten Sleep is at the base of the Big Horn Mountains in north-central Wyoming. What might account for the difference in their average temperatures?

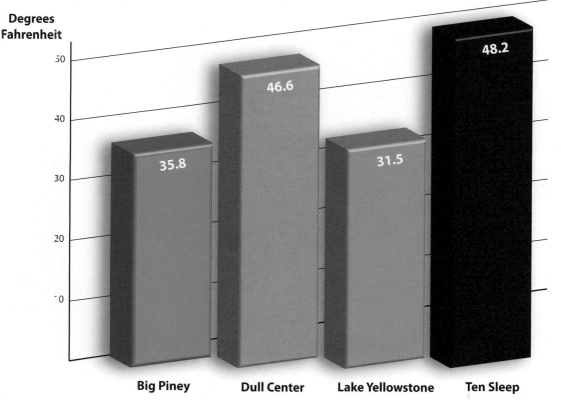

Natural Resources

Wyoming's lumber companies log Douglas firs, ponderosa pines, and lodgepole pines. Trees logged in Wyoming are used to make plywood, pulp, and paper products.

This Western state is rich in mineral resources. Wyoming is the nation's leader in trona mining. Trona is made up mostly of sodium carbonate. Chemicals made from trona are used to produce soap, baking soda, products used to purify water, and many other items. The state as a whole produces about 18 million tons of trona per year. Wyoming's trona industry employs about 3,000 people.

Large deposits of bentonite are also found in the state. Bentonite is an ingredient in glue, cosmetics, toothpaste, and paint. Other natural resources found in Wyoming include coal, natural gas, uranium, iron ore, limestone, and gypsum.

Bloodstone is green jasper with spots of iron oxide. It is used in jewelry. Wyoming is a leading source of gemstones in the United States. Jade, moss agate, ruby, jasper, star sapphire, and bloodstone are all found in the state.

In the Powder River Basin, the coalfield produces more coal than any other field in the United States. Crude oil or natural gas is drilled in almost all of Wyoming's 23 counties. In a typical year, the state produces about 50 million barrels of crude oil, making it the seventh-largest oil-producing state. In 2010, Wyoming produced more natural gas than any other state except Texas.

The wind is also a valuable natural resource. The U.S. Energy Information Administration has called southern Wyoming one of the best places in the nation for generating electricity using wind power.

Wyoming grows plenty of hay, barley, wheat, beets, and corn. However, livestock is the biggest part of state agriculture. In recent years, sales of livestock have been worth $60 billion and more.

Plants

Trees of many kinds grow in the mountains and along the streams of Wyoming. Most are conifers, which are cone-producing trees. The lodgepole pine grows well in the higher mountains of Wyoming, where the climate is cool and wet. Douglas fir trees are plentiful, and aspens, cottonwoods, and willows are also common.

About four-fifths of the land is covered with grasses and the types of shrubs that survive in desert or desertlike conditions. Mosses, **lichens**, and wildflowers, such as Indian paintbrush and forget-me-nots, are also found in Wyoming. Sagebrush and western wheatgrass flourish in the lowlands. The driest regions of the state are home to plants that require little water to grow, such as yuccas and cacti.

INDIAN PAINTBRUSH

GLACIER LILY

The Indian paintbrush is Wyoming's state flower. It is also known as the painted cup.

Glacier lilies are bright spring flowers found at elevations above 7,500 feet.

SAGEBRUSH

Sagebrush is the main vegetation found in the Wyoming Basin Shrub Steppe, an area drained by the Green, Wind, Bighorn, and North Platte rivers.

LODGEPOLE PINE

Lodgepole pines are mainly found in the south-central area of the state.

The Northern Prairie Wildlife Research Center tracks the occurrence of rare plants in four districts of the state. As the information is updated, it allows state and federal agencies to make better decisions about plants that need protection.

Bighorn National Forest is the state's largest preserve of trees. Most of the tree species found in the state can be found within the protected forest.

The higher the elevation, the shorter the shrubs. The plants in the alpine zone, above 10,000 feet, adapt to the cold and wind by growing close to the ground.

Most of the wildflowers that grow in Wyoming are found at elevations between 7,000 and 10,000 feet above sea level.

Animals

Wyoming has more pronghorns than anyplace else in the world. Pronghorns, which are sometimes called antelope, although they are not related, are more numerous than people in Wyoming. The state also has the world's largest elk herd. Thousands of elk spend their winters at the National Elk Refuge. Mule deer are found throughout the state, and white-tailed deer live in the Black Hills area. Moose wander the northwestern part of the state, and herds of bison, or buffalo, roam Yellowstone and Grand Teton national parks. Bighorn sheep live in the northern part of the state. Wyoming also has rabbits, coyotes, and bobcats living within its borders.

Many birds make their home in Wyoming. The sage grouse lives throughout the state. Other birds in Wyoming include pheasants, partridges, wild turkeys, white pelicans, trumpeter swans, and whistler swans. Bass, walleye, perch, channel catfish, trout, and many other species of fish swim in Wyoming's rivers and lakes.

SAGE GROUSE

Adult sage grouse are the largest of North American grouse species. The sage grouse was recently put under state protection to increase its numbers.

PRONGHORN

Pronghorns can run at speeds of about 60 miles per hour. Nearly half of all pronghorns in North America are found in Wyoming.

ELK

Elk from the National Elk Refuge at Jackson Hole are sent to other parts of the country to help other herds grow bigger and stronger.

HORNED TOAD

The state reptile is the horned toad. The "toad" is actually a lizard.

About 3,000 bison can be found in Yellowstone National Park in a typical year.

Black bears roam much of Wyoming's forested regions.

Grizzly bears live in Yellowstone National Park and the surrounding region. The bears are found in higher mountain and wilderness areas. The average weight of grizzly bears is 800 pounds. They range in height from 5 to 8 feet tall.

Tourism

Yellowstone National Park is Wyoming's most popular tourist destination. The park, which extends into Montana and Idaho, is known for its geysers, which are hot springs that shoot jets of hot water and steam into the air. The water is forced out from superheated underground mineral springs.

The park contains the greatest concentration of geysers in the world. The best-known geyser in Yellowstone is Old Faithful, whose blasts can last for up to five minutes and can reach more than 170 feet in height.

Grand Teton National Park rivals Yellowstone as the most picturesque park in Wyoming. Located in northwestern Wyoming, Grand Teton National Park features some of the youngest mountains in the Rockies. The park has more than 200 miles of trails.

WYOMING DINOSAUR CENTER

Visitors to the Wyoming Dinosaur Center in Thermopolis can tour the museum or participate in an archaeological dig. The museum has dozens of full-size skeletons.

OLD FAITHFUL

Old Faithful expels between 3,700 and 8,400 gallons of hot water per eruption.

FORT LARAMIE

Fort Laramie National Historic Site is another popular destination in Wyoming. Significant people in the history of the Old West who passed through the fort include Kit Carson, Crazy Horse, and Wyatt Earp.

DUDE RANCHES

Dude ranches are resorts that offer visitors a variety of ranching experiences. Most of these vacation destinations offer a personal horse for the time of a visitor's stay.

Thermopolis has one of the world's largest natural hot springs. Even in winter, tourists can swim and relax in the warm mineral pools.

About 7 million people visit Wyoming each year. Tourism is a leading industry in the state, generating more than $2 billion in annual revenue.

Visitors have enjoyed Cheyenne Frontier Days since 1897. Every summer the city celebrates its history with parades, chuck-wagon cook-offs, and rodeos.

Industry

Mining is Wyoming's most important industry. The state produces about 40 percent of the nation's coal. A portion of the state's coal is burned to create electricity, which is used in Wyoming and also sold to other states. People in Wyoming pay less for electricity than many other Americans do, in part because the state does not have a number of pollution regulations that other states enforce.

Industries in Wyoming
Value of Goods and Services in Millions of Dollars

The mining of fuels such as coal, oil, and natural gas accounts for a significant amount of the state's economy. These fuels are nonrenewable. Once they have been used, they are gone. How might Wyoming make the best use of these resources and protect its economy over time?

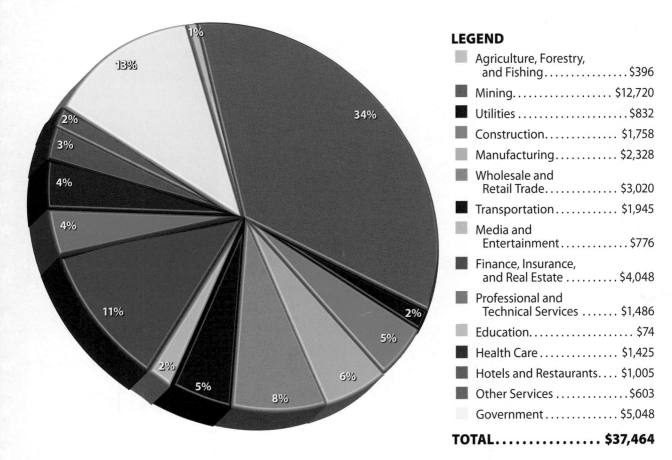

LEGEND

Agriculture, Forestry, and Fishing	$396
Mining	$12,720
Utilities	$832
Construction	$1,758
Manufacturing	$2,328
Wholesale and Retail Trade	$3,020
Transportation	$1,945
Media and Entertainment	$776
Finance, Insurance, and Real Estate	$4,048
Professional and Technical Services	$1,486
Education	$74
Health Care	$1,425
Hotels and Restaurants	$1,005
Other Services	$603
Government	$5,048
TOTAL	**$37,464**

Wyoming's natural gas and oil production protected it during a recent economic downturn in the rest of the country. Sublette County, which has two of the nation's biggest natural gas fields, has had the lowest unemployment rate in the nation. Manufacturing plants utilize the raw materials mined in the state. The refining of petroleum and the processing of coal are especially important. Wyoming's chemical plants produce fertilizers and other agricultural chemicals.

Another major industry is tourism. Overall, the state's service industries, including tourism, provide many of the jobs in the state. In service industries, workers help or provide a service for other people. People who work in banks, hospitals, stores, and restaurants are all service workers.

Wyoming has approximately 2,000 miles of railroads. Raw materials such as coal are often shipped by rail.

In 2010, a total of 314,000 acres of land in Wyoming were leased to oil and gas companies.

Many of the new oil wells being drilled in the state rely on fracturing, also known as fracking. That is a process in which sand, water, and chemicals are flushed through rock so the oil products can rush up.

Oil and gas producers are looking for cost-effective ways to treat the water used in fracking to make it clean enough for other uses. In the meantime, most of it is being sent to dumping grounds.

Wyoming uses the water power of its rivers to produce electricity. Major **hydroelectric** plants are located on the Green, North Platte, Wind, Shoshone, and Big Horn rivers. Water-generated electricity accounts for about 2 percent of the total electricity produced in the state.

Goods and Services

Almost all of the agricultural land in Wyoming is used for ranching. Cattle and sheep are important to the state's economy. The sheep are raised mainly for wool, and Wyoming is a national leader in wool production.

Wyoming has little cropland because there is not enough precipitation to grow most crops. Farms that are **irrigated** can grow beans, potatoes, corn, and sugar beets. However, some land is dry-farmed for crops such as barley, wheat, and hay. Rather than relying on irrigation, this type of farming usually involves plowing deep into the earth and planting seed in the fall, when it is cooler.

The Francis E. Warren Air Force Base serves as the home of the 90th Missile Wing, the nation's largest strategic missile unit.

Wyoming's ranchers work together in groups such as the Wyoming Stock Growers Association to share management ideas and to lobby legislators.

Various types of machinery, such as construction and farm equipment, are produced in Wyoming's factories. Food processing plants produce dairy and bakery items. Wyoming also manufactures stone, clay, and glass products.

About one-half of Wyoming's workers are employed in the service sector. A large percentage of service workers are employed by the federal government, the state government, or local governments. Some of these people work in the national forests and parks. Others work at the Francis E. Warren Air Force Base near Cheyenne.

About half of Wyoming's land is owned by the state or federal government.

Cattle are the number one agricultural product in the state. Hay is second. Hogs are third. Sheep and lambs are fourth.

The state became a center for ranching after the railroads came through in the mid-to-late 1800s. The railway made it easier to ship beef and other related products.

Wyoming has about 11,000 farms and ranches.

Approximately 10,000 undergraduate students attend the University of Wyoming, or UW. The university opened in Laramie in 1887, when Wyoming was still a territory. It is the state's only four-year institution of higher education and research. UW athletic teams are called the Cowboys. They play in the Mountain West Conference.

American Indians

I t is believed that people were living in what is now Wyoming at least 12,000 years ago or more. These early residents lived in caves and hunted big game, such as **mammoths** and bison. Some of these groups left behind pictures that were carved and painted onto rocks.

Over time many American Indian groups settled in Wyoming. One of the largest was the Shoshone. Other American Indian communities included the Arapaho, Crow, Cheyenne, Blackfoot, Ute, and Bannock. Most of the groups were nomadic, moving frequently to hunt animals, especially bison.

When European explorers first began to visit the area, Wyoming's population was probably less than 10,000. The explorers were followed by fur trappers and traders.

The lives of the American Indians in the area changed drastically in the 1800s as growing numbers of settlers of European descent arrived.

The name Shoshone means "The Valley People." Early on, the Shoshone lived in tepees made of animal hide stretched over branches and poles.

At first relations between the American Indians and the settlers were peaceful, and the groups traded with each other. However, American Indians began to die from smallpox and other diseases carried by the new arrivals. In addition, the settlers took over or destroyed much of the American Indian hunting grounds. Bitter fighting erupted over control of the land. By the late 1800s most of the American Indians had been driven out of the region.

Early American Indians built a "medicine wheel" near Lovell. The wheel might have been used as a giant calendar. The site is considered sacred and is still used for religious ceremonies.

Sacagawea was a Shoshone woman who acted as an important guide and interpreter for the **expedition** led by U.S. explorers Meriwether Lewis and William Clark into the American West. Some scholars believe she died at Fort Manuel in what is now South Dakota in 1812. Others claim that she died on Wyoming's Wind River Indian Reservation in 1884.

The Arapaho divided into southern and northern groups in the 1800s.

The name "Wyoming" originally comes from the Lenape people and a word meaning something like "at the large plains." The Lenape did not live in Wyoming, but their word was borrowed.

Explorers

It is believed that the first Europeans to explore what is now Wyoming were the French Canadian brothers François and Louis Joseph de Vérendrye. They visited the area in 1743 while unsuccessfully searching for a route to the Pacific Ocean. In the early 1800s, John Colter entered the region. He had been a member of the Lewis and Clark Expedition but left to become a fur trapper and trader.

In the early 1800s hundreds of men traveled to Wyoming to work as trappers and to trade with the American Indians for valuable furs. These trappers, called mountain men, assembled each year at a gathering called a **rendezvous**. They traded with American Indians, held great feasts, played games, sang songs, and danced. Eventually forts were built, and they became the meeting places. A typical early rendezvous lasted a couple of days, while later ones were often several months long.

The Green River Rendezvous was an important annual meeting of Wyoming's trappers, traders, and American Indians. The last rendezvous was held in 1840. By that time, so many beavers had been hunted for their fur, that the beaver population in the region had greatly declined.

Mormons traveled to the region in large numbers in the mid-1800s. They settled near Fort Bridger on the Green River.

Timeline of Settlement

Early Explorers and Traders

1743 Brothers François and Louis Joseph de La Vérendrye reach what is now Wyoming. They are the first Europeans to travel this far northwest.

1807 John Colter is the first explorer to see and describe the geysers at Yellowstone.

1812 Robert Stuart builds the first known cabin in the region, on the North Platte River near Bessemer Bend.

1825 The time in the fur trade known as the rendezvous period begins. The majority of Wyoming trappers work for fur companies, which ship most of the furs to Europe. "Free trappers" trade bear and other furs to the highest bidder.

First Settlements

1834 Fort Laramie is established as the first permanent trading post.

1842 Captain John C. Frémont makes his first expedition to Wyoming.

1843 Fort Bridger, the second permanent settlement, is established.

1852 The first school for children opens at Fort Laramie.

Territory and Statehood

1868 The Wyoming Territory is established. The next year, the first governor, John A. Campbell, takes office.

1886 The Northwestern Railroad reaches the eastern edge of Wyoming. The Cheyenne and Northern Railway reaches Douglas.

1889 The Wyoming Constitutional Convention is held.

1890 In July, President Benjamin Harrison signs the act that admits Wyoming to the Union as the 44th state.

Early Settlers

Many settlers traveled through Wyoming on the Oregon Trail. Fort Laramie was the last major place to rest and purchase supplies before entering the mountains. Once through the mountains, the settlers reached Independence Rock, where they carved their names and messages into the stone. This was their way of letting friends and family who followed know that they had made it through the mountains safely.

Map of Settlements and Resources in Early Wyoming

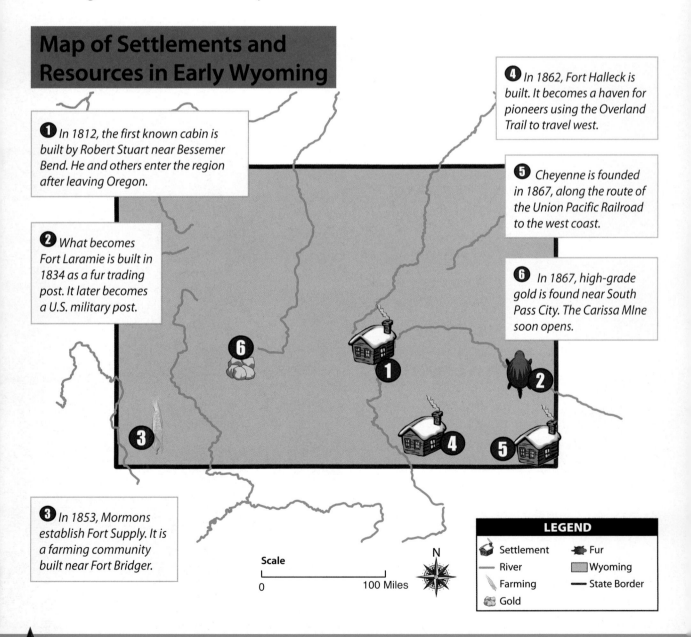

❶ *In 1812, the first known cabin is built by Robert Stuart near Bessemer Bend. He and others enter the region after leaving Oregon.*

❷ *What becomes Fort Laramie is built in 1834 as a fur trading post. It later becomes a U.S. military post.*

❸ *In 1853, Mormons establish Fort Supply. It is a farming community built near Fort Bridger.*

❹ *In 1862, Fort Halleck is built. It becomes a haven for pioneers using the Overland Trail to travel west.*

❺ *Cheyenne is founded in 1867, along the route of the Union Pacific Railroad to the west coast.*

❻ *In 1867, high-grade gold is found near South Pass City. The Carissa MIne soon opens.*

Scale

0   100 Miles

N

LEGEND	
Settlement	Fur
River	Wyoming
Farming	State Border
Gold	

Some of the people who entered Wyoming decided to settle in the area. The settlers often killed or drove away animals that the American Indians depended on for food. There were many battles over the years. In 1851, American Indians in Wyoming began signing a series of peace **treaties** with the U.S. government. According to the treaties, the American Indians would allow forts, roads, and railroads to be built in exchange for land.

In 1867 the first train of the Union Pacific Railroad reached Cheyenne. Cities sprang up along the new railroad lines, and people came to work on the railroads. Others arrived to purchase cheap land or to open businesses.

The Union Pacific Railroad arrived in the 1860s. The Northwestern and the Cheyenne and Northern railroads entered the state nearly 20 years later, further establishing Wyoming as a place of commerce.

I DIDN'T KNOW THAT!

After 1840 many mountain men stayed in Wyoming and worked as guides. Their knowledge of the region was invaluable to expeditions.

Mountain men often had interesting names such as Jeremiah "Liver Eating" Johnston and Thomas "Broken Hand" Fitzpatrick.

The first oil well in Wyoming was drilled in 1884.

Scholars estimate that one out of every 10 travelers died on the Oregon Trail, usually from **cholera**, poor living conditions, or accidental gunshots.

Independence Rock has been nicknamed the Great Register of the Desert because more than 5,000 names have been carved onto its surface.

The discovery of gold in the South Pass area led to a gold rush in the late 1860s.

Many cattle drives passed through Wyoming in the mid-to-late 1800s. During cattle drives, cowboys led cattle from ranches to rail yards. The trails were sometimes 20 miles wide.

Notable People

Wyoming has had its share of people who made exceptional contributions to their state and nation. Notable Wyomingites have played key roles in the exploration and settlement of the American West. Others have served in important government positions and as leaders in other fields.

**FRANCIS E. WARREN
(1844–1929)**

Francis Warren received the Congressional Medal of Honor for his bravery in the Civil War. He moved to Wyoming in 1868, where he pursued interests in ranching and real estate. In the years that followed, he served in a variety of public capacities for the territory and then the state. He was a senator for the territory, Cheyenne city councilman and mayor, treasurer for the territory, territorial governor, and state governor. Warren then spent many years in Washington, D.C., as a U.S. senator for Wyoming, a role he was fulfilling on the day of his death.

**JOSEPH M. CAREY
(1845–1924)**

Joseph M. Carey campaigned for presidential candidate Ulysses S. Grant. During Grant's presidency, he was appointed U.S. district attorney for Wyoming. Carey also served as an associate justice on the Wyoming Supreme Court. After a stint in ranching, he returned to public life as the mayor of Cheyenne. Eventually he served as the U.S. congressional delegate for the Territory of Wyoming. It was Carey who wrote the bill that admitted Wyoming to statehood. After Wyoming became a state, he was a U.S. senator and a state governor.

WILLIAM F. CODY (1846–1917)

William Frederick Cody delivered mail for the **Pony Express**. After Civil War service, he was a U.S. Army scout. He hunted buffalo to feed railway crews, attaining celebrity status as "Buffalo Bill." Newspapers featured his dramatic fights with American Indians, and he used his fame to start a traveling show about the Wild West. One of his homes was in Cody.

NELLIE TAYLOR ROSS (1876–1977)

During the 1924 election for governor, Nellie Taylor Ross defeated her rival by more than 8,000 votes to become the first female governor of any U.S. state. In 1933, President Franklin Roosevelt named her the director of the U.S. Mint, another "first" for a woman.

ANNE GORSUCH BURFORD (1942–2004)

Anne Gorsuch Burford was born in Casper. She was appointed the administrator of the Environmental Protection Agency when Ronald Reagan was president. Burford, a Conservative, served in the Colorado House of Representatives before going to Washington, D.C.

I DIDN'T KNOW THAT!

Jedediah Smith (1799–1831) joined General William Ashley on an expedition to explore the Upper Missouri River at age 22. A year later, Smith blazed a trail through the South Pass, leading the way for settlement in the West. He became a mountain man, traveling throughout Wyoming and other western territories as a partner in two fur-trading companies.

Dick Cheney (1941–) held important positions in the administrations of both Presidents Bush. He was secretary of defense during the administration of George H. W. Bush and vice president during the administration of George W. Bush. Cheney grew up in Casper. Before becoming secretary of defense, he served six terms in the U.S. House of Representatives.

Population

Wyoming has the smallest population of all the 50 states. In the 2010 Census, 563,626 people called the Equality State home. Cheyenne is the largest city, with a population of about 57,000. Casper follows closely behind, with a population of about 55,000. Other major cities are Laramie, Gillette, Rock Springs, and Sheridan. Cities and towns play an important role in Wyoming. With so few people and so much land, towns are a place for people to meet and stay in touch with their distant neighbors. Wyoming has a **population density** of only about six people per square mile. The national average is approximately 87 people per square mile.

Wyoming Population 1950–2010

Wyoming's population grew by more than 14 percent from 2000 to 2010, almost one and a half times the national average. What are some reasons for the recent dramatic population growth in the state?

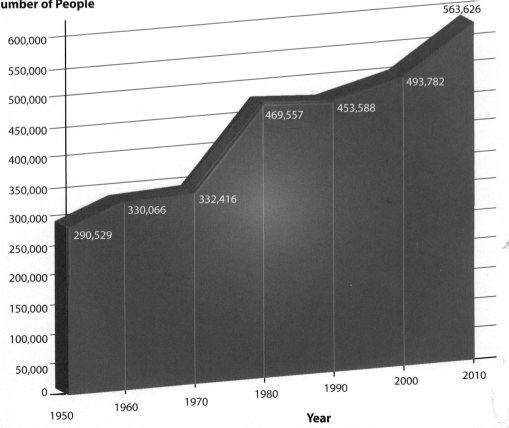

Number of People

- 290,529 (1950)
- 330,066 (1960)
- 332,416 (1970)
- 469,557 (1980)
- 453,588 (1990)
- 493,782 (2000)
- 563,626 (2010)

Year

The state's population is projected to grow to 571,280 by 2018.

Nearly 98 out of every 100 Wyomingites were born in the United States. Most are of European **heritage**. The largest groups are people of German, English, and Irish descent.

In the state of Wyoming, the population that lives outside metropolitan centers is much larger than the population inside metropolitan centers.

Approximately 87,500 students are enrolled in Wyoming's public schools. The Laramie and Natrona districts have the most students.

The population of the Wind River Indian Reservation includes approximately 2,500 Shoshone and 5,000 Arapaho Indians. However, visitors can drive for miles without seeing people because the inhabitants live on 2.2 million acres.

The legislature began meeting in the capitol when Wyoming was still a territory. Wyoming legislators were the first to grant women the right to vote and to hold public office. Wyoming was also the first state to allow women to serve on juries.

Politics and Government

Wyoming's state government is divided into three branches. As in other states, they are the legislative, the executive, and the judicial branches. The legislative branch creates laws for the state and consists of a House of Representatives and a Senate. There are 30 state senators elected to four-year terms and 60 representatives elected to two-year terms. The executive branch of government enforces state laws. It is headed by the governor. Other important executive branch officials include the state auditor, treasurer, superintendent of public instruction, and secretary of state. All are elected to four-year terms. The judicial branch is made up of the state's courts. The Supreme Court, the state's highest court, has five justices who serve eight-year terms.

Wyoming is divided into 23 counties. Each county is governed by a board of commissioners. The commissioners are elected to four-year terms.

The city of Cheyenne is located in Laramie County. The city has a mayor-council form of government. Nine council members are elected for four-year terms, which are staggered.

Cultural Groups

Wyoming's American Indians have a rich cultural heritage. Every year they hold powwows to celebrate their history and traditions. Powwows were traditionally held to celebrate such events as major hunts and marriage ceremonies. Today, they can range from family reunions to major cultural events that attract American Indians from all over the country.

The Shoshone and Arapaho hold many powwows during the summer on the Wind River Indian Reservation. Dancing competitions are popular events at these powwows. Visitors to these celebrations can also experience traditional American Indian arts, crafts, and foods. In addition, the reservation has several cultural centers that allow visitors to learn more about American Indian customs and history.

More than 10 different American Indian groups once lived in Wyoming, including the Cheyenne and the Sioux. Today, the main groups are the Shoshone and Arapaho.

Wyoming takes pride in its cowboy culture. The rodeo was designated the official state sport in 2003. The Wyoming state quarter features a cowboy on a horse.

Cowboys have played an important role in Wyoming's history, and cowboy culture has remained an important aspect of Wyoming life. Many communities celebrate the state's ranching heritage with rodeos.

Cowboy ballads are the official folk music of Wyoming. Many of the original ballads came from the cowboys who took part in the cattle drives of the late 1800s. Today traditional cowboy music is still sung on the range and can be heard at county fairs and other state celebrations. Cowboy poetry contests and readings are another celebration of cowboy tradition.

The Wind River Indian Reservation was the only reservation in the country where American Indians were allowed to choose the land they lived on.

Originally established in 1863 for the Shoshone tribe, the Wind River Indian Reservation later became home to the Arapaho as well.

Cody calls itself the Rodeo Capital of the World. The town holds a rodeo every night during the summer.

Cowboy culture is so ingrained in Wyoming that the state has a registered trademark known as the bucking horse and rider.

Wyoming Pioneer Memorial Museum in Douglas displays artifacts from the early settlers in Wyoming.

The Wyoming Department of State Parks and Cultural Resources is looking at ways to better promote Wyoming's Western culture. Money is being used to promote sites attractive to "rut nuts," or people who like to follow historic trails, and "culture vultures," people who enjoy regional festivals.

Arts and Entertainment

Festivals and other cultural events define the seasons in Wyoming. The town of Douglas hosts the popular Wyoming State Fair each summer. In addition to typical rodeo events, the fair features a demolition derby and pig-wrestling contests. Sheridan hosts the Big Horn Mountain Festival, featuring **acoustic**, folk, bluegrass, and other traditional music.

Jackson Pollock was born in Cody in 1912. Pollock was one of the leading artists of the abstract expressionist movement. He developed a form of painting in which he dripped and splattered paint, sand, and even broken glass on a canvas placed on the floor. It became known as action painting, in which the act is as important as the finished work.

The University of Wyoming has classical music groups, including a symphony orchestra and a choir. The Grand Teton Music Festival, held annually in Jackson Hole, typically features some 40 concerts. Every Fourth of July, Jackson Hole holds a free outdoor concert as part of the festival. The concert attracts thousands of people. Also associated with the event is the Festival Orchestra, an ensemble featuring some of the country's leading classical musicians.

Museums offer year-round entertainment. The National Museum of Wildlife Art in Jackson Hole contains about 5,000 works of art in its collection, many of which were inspired by Wyoming. Buffalo Bill Cody founded the town of Cody. The town's Buffalo Bill Historical Center features a gallery of Western art, several museums, and a research library. A museum dedicated to Buffalo Bill has cowboy gear, firearms, and other artifacts from his life.

The Jackson Hole Fall Arts Festival features contemporary, landscape, wildlife, American Indian, and Western art installations.

Sports

Wyoming is known for many sports, including rock-climbing and ballooning, but it is best known for rodeo sports. Rodeo events are considered some of the most dangerous in the world. Popular events include saddle **bronco** riding, bareback bronco riding, bull riding, steer wrestling, and calf roping. In bull riding, contestants try to remain on a bucking bull. In steer wrestling, or bulldogging, competitors jump from their horse onto a steer, grab it by the horns, and then pin it to the ground. During calf-roping and steer-roping contests, participants race to see how quickly and how well they can capture and tie up the animals.

At Medicine Bow-Routt National Forest near Laramie, the Vedauwoo rocks attract climbers. The area is also a destination for hiking and camping.

Both Yellowstone National Park and Grand Teton National Park provide many opportunities for outdoor recreation. Hiking, camping, and nature walks are popular in the forests and mountains of Yellowstone, and Grand Teton is an ideal location for backpacking, climbing, canoeing, and fishing.

Hunting is yet another popular sport in Wyoming. Men and women can apply for licenses to hunt elk, deer, antelope, moose, bighorn sheep, and other animals.

In the winter months, skiing and snowshoeing are common activities in Grand Teton National Park. Wyoming has a number of popular ski resorts. Snowmobiling and sled-dog racing are also popular winter pursuits.

The University of Wyoming football squad keeps the state's sports fans cheering. The University of Wyoming has teams in a number of sports, including men's and women's basketball, women's volleyball, swimming, and track. The school also has a rodeo club.

I DIDN'T KNOW THAT!

Wyoming is a destination for hang gliders. There are plenty of **thermals** to ride.

Sportscaster Curt Gowdy was born in Wyoming. He was the radio voice of the New York Yankees and the Boston Red Sox, and he also broadcast football and baseball games on national television. In 1981 he was inducted into the Sports Broadcasters Hall of Fame.

Wyoming has 15,846 miles of fishing streams and 297,633 acres of fishing lakes. A total of 3,400 lakes, ponds, and reservoirs are home to more than 75 types of fish.

Volksmarches, which translates as "people walks," are long hikes through the beautiful Wyoming scenery.

National Averages Comparison

T he United States is a federal republic, consisting of fifty states and the District of Columbia. Alaska and Hawai'i are the only non-contiguous, or non-touching, states in the nation. Today, the United States of America is the third-largest country in the world in population. The United States Census Bureau takes a census, or count of all the people, every ten years. It also regularly collects other kinds of data about the population and the economy. How does Wyoming compare to the national average?

Comparison Chart

United States 2010 Census Data *	USA	Wyoming
Admission to Union	NA	July 10, 1890
Land Area (in square miles)	3,537,438.44	97,100.40
Population Total	308,745,538	563,626
Population Density (people per square mile)	87.28	5.80
Population Percentage Change (April 1, 2000, to April 1, 2010)	9.7%	14.1%
White Persons (percent)	72.4%	90.7%
Black Persons (percent)	12.6%	0.8%
American Indian and Alaska Native Persons (percent)	0.9%	2.4%
Asian Persons (percent)	4.8%	0.8%
Native Hawaiian and Other Pacific Islander Persons (percent)	0.2%	0.1%
Some Other Race (percent)	6.2%	3.0%
Persons Reporting Two or More Races (percent)	2.9%	2.2%
Persons of Hispanic or Latino Origin (percent)	16.3%	8.9%
Not of Hispanic or Latino Origin (percent)	83.7%	91.1%
Median Household Income	$52,029	$54,735
Percentage of People Age 25 or Over Who Have Graduated from High School	80.4%	87.9%

*All figures are based on the 2010 United States Census, with the exception of the last two items.

How to Improve My Community

Strong communities make strong states. Think about what features are important in your community. What do you value? Education? Health? Forests? Safety? Beautiful spaces? Government works to help citizens create ideal living conditions that are fair to all by providing services in communities. Consider what changes you could make in your community. How would they improve your state as a whole? Using this concept web as a guide, write a report that outlines the features you think are most important in your community and what improvements could be made. A strong state needs strong communities.

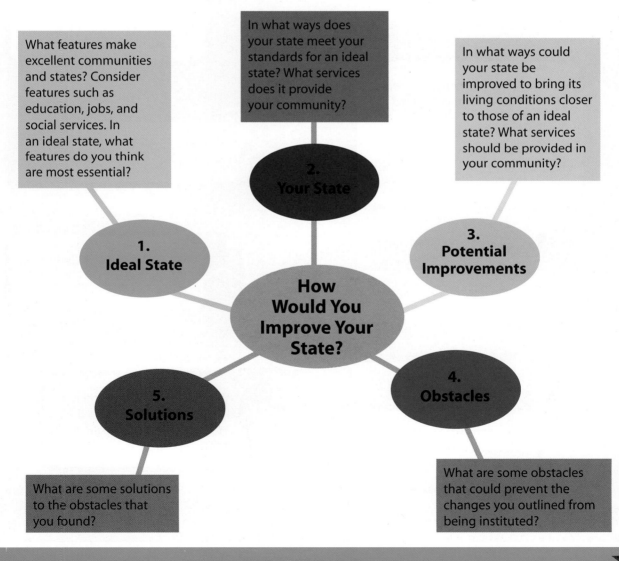

What features make excellent communities and states? Consider features such as education, jobs, and social services. In an ideal state, what features do you think are most essential?

In what ways does your state meet your standards for an ideal state? What services does it provide your community?

In what ways could your state be improved to bring its living conditions closer to those of an ideal state? What services should be provided in your community?

2.
Your State

3.
Potential Improvements

1.
Ideal State

How Would You Improve Your State?

4.
Obstacles

5.
Solutions

What are some solutions to the obstacles that you found?

What are some obstacles that could prevent the changes you outlined from being instituted?

Exercise Your Mind!

Think about these questions and then use your research skills to find the answers and learn more fascinating facts about Wyoming. A teacher, librarian, or parent may be able to help you locate the best sources to use in your research.

1 Which famous store got its start in Kemmerer?

2 Robert LeRoy Parker was the real name of which famous outlaw?

a. The Sundance Kid
b. Jesse James
c. Butch Cassidy
d. Billy the Kid

3 Who invented the dude ranch?

4 True or False? Most of the area that is now Wyoming was acquired from France.

5 Which U.S. vice president is associated with Wyoming?

a. Dan Quayle
b. Dick Cheney
c. Al Gore
d. Walter Mondale

6 What is the town of Afton known for?

7 Which horse is the model for the Bucking Horse and Rider trademark?

8 Which well-known Wyoming landmark was featured in the 1977 movie *Close Encounters of the Third Kind*?

Words to Know

acoustic: of or relating to a musical instrument that is not electric

bronco: a rodeo horse that tries to buck off a rider

capitol: building for the legislature

cholera: an infectious disease, characterized by cramps and vomiting, which is often spread through dirty water

expedition: a journey made for exploration

heritage: traditions that result from a person's natural situation

hydroelectric: of or relating to the generation of electricity from water power

irrigated: watered by artificial means

lichens: crusty growth found on rocks or tree trunks which results from fungus growing with algae

magnate: person who has great influence in industry or business

mammoths: prehistoric fur-covered elephant-like animals

Mormon: of or relating to the Church of Jesus Christ of Latter-day Saints

Pony Express: an early system for transporting mail using horses and riders

population density: the average number of people per unit of area

rendezvous: French for "a meeting"

thermals: updrafts of air in the lower atmosphere created by uneven warming on the surface of Earth

treaties: formal agreements between two governments

Index

Log on to www.av2books.com

AV² by Weigl brings you media enhanced books that support active learning. Go to www.av2books.com, and enter the special code found on page 2 of this book. You will gain access to enriched and enhanced content that supplements and complements this book. Content includes video, audio, web links, quizzes, a slide show, and activities.

Audio
Listen to sections of the book read aloud.

Video
Watch informative video clips.

Embedded Weblinks
Gain additional information for research.

Try This!
Complete activities and hands-on experiments.

WHAT'S ONLINE?

Try This!	Embedded Weblinks	Video	EXTRA FEATURES
Test your knowledge of the state in a mapping activity.	Discover more attractions in Wyoming.	Watch a video introduction to Wyoming.	**Audio** Listen to sections of the book read aloud.
Find out more about precipitation in your city.	Learn more about the history of the state.	Watch a video about the features of the state.	**Key Words** Study vocabulary, and complete a matching word activity.
Plan what attractions you would like to visit in the state.	Learn the full lyrics of the state song.		
Learn more about the early natural resources of the state.			**Slide Show** View images and captions, and prepare a presentation.
Write a biography about a notable resident of Wyoming.			
Complete an educational census activity.			**Quizzes** Test your knowledge.

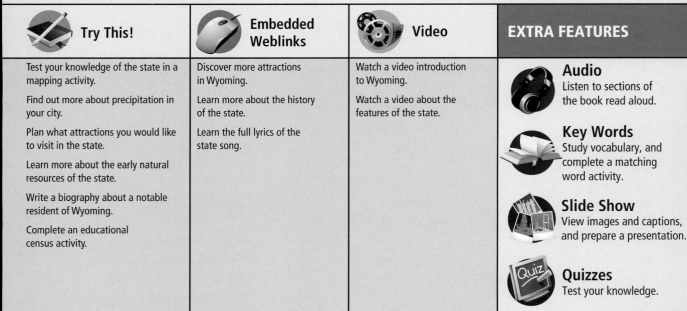

AV² was built to bridge the gap between print and digital. We encourage you to tell us what you like and what you want to see in the future.
Sign up to be an AV² Ambassador at www.av2books.com/ambassador.